Born in 2001

by

Kerry Butters.

Born in 2001

Millennium:	**3rd millennium**
Centuries:	20th century – **21st century** – 22nd century
Decades:	1970s 1980s 1990s – **2000s** – 2010s 2020s 2030s
Years:	1998 1999 2000 – **2001** – 2002 2003 2004

2001 (MMI) was a common year starting on Monday (dominical letter G) of the Gregorian calendar, the 2001st year of the Common Era (CE) and *Anno Domini* (AD) designations, the 1st year of the 3rd millennium, the 1st year of the 21st century, and the 2nd year of the 2000s decade.

2001 was designated as:

International Year of Volunteers

Contents

- 1 Events
- 2 Births
- 3 Deaths
- 4 Nobel Prizes
- 5 In fiction
- 6 In the News

Events

January

- January 10 – The U.S. Federal Trade Commission approves the merger of America Online and Time Warner to form AOL Time Warner.
- January 13 – A 7.6 magnitude earthquake hits all of El Salvador, killing at least 800 people and leaving thousands homeless.
- January 15 – Wikipedia launches.
- January 20
    - George W. Bush is sworn into office, succeeding Bill Clinton as President of the United States, over candidate contender Al Gore in the disputed U.S. presidential election, 2000.
    - Impeachment proceedings against Philippine President Joseph Estrada, accused of playing Jueteng, end preeminently and trigger the second EDSA People Power Revolution or People Power II. His Vice-President Gloria Macapagal-Arroyo succeeds him as the 14th President of the Republic.
- January 23 – The Tiananmen Square self-immolation incident occurs.
- January 26 – An earthquake hits Gujarat, India, killing almost 20,000.
- January 31 – The Congressional Budget Office of the United States forecasts a $5,600,000,000,000 budget surplus for the next 10 years.

February

- February 9 – The submarine USS *Greeneville* accidentally strikes and sinks the Japanese fishing vessel *Ehime-Maru* near Hawaii.
- February 12 – The NEAR Shoemaker spacecraft touches down in the "saddle" region of 433 Eros, becoming the first spacecraft to land on an asteroid.
- February 13 – A 6.6 magnitude earthquake hits El Salvador, killing at least 400.
- February 16 – Iraq disarmament crisis: British and U.S. forces carry out bombing raids, attempting to disable Iraq's air defense network.
- February 18 – FBI agent Robert Hanssen is arrested and charged with spying for Russia for 25 years.
- February 20 – The 2001 UK foot-and-mouth crisis begins.
- February 28 – The Great Heck rail crash occurs.

March

- March 2 – The Taliban begins destruction of the Bamiyan Buddhas.
- March 4 – A bomb explodes at BBC Television Centre in London, UK.
- March 23
  - The deorbit of Russian space station Mir is carried out near Nadi, Fiji, with Mir falling into the Pacific Ocean.
  - The World Wrestling Federation (WWF/now WWE) purchases rival organization World Championship Wrestling (WCW) for an estimated US$7 million.
- March 24 - The first release of Mac OS X is released as the successor to Mac OS 9 and the Mac OS X Public Beta, which would not cease to function until May 14.

April

- April 1
  - Hainan Island incident: A Chinese fighter jet bumps into a U.S. EP-3E surveillance aircraft, which is forced to make an emergency landing in Hainan, China. The U.S. crew is detained for 10 days and the F-8 Chinese pilot, Wang Wei, goes missing and is presumed dead.
  - Former Federal Republic of Yugoslavia President Slobodan Milošević surrenders to police special forces, to be tried on charges of war crimes.
  - In the Netherlands, the Act on the Opening up of Marriage goes into effect. The Act allows same-sex couples to marry legally for the first time in the world since the reign of Nero.
- April 28 – *Soyuz TM-32* lifts off from the Baikonur Cosmodrome, carrying the first space tourist, American Dennis Tito.

May

- May 6 – Space tourist Dennis Tito returns to Earth aboard *Soyuz TM-31*. (*Soyuz TM-32* is left docked at the International Space Station as a new lifeboat.)
- May 7 – In Banja Luka, Bosnia and Herzegovina, an attempt is made to reconstruct the Ferhadija mosque. However, the ceremony results in mass riots by Serb nationalists, who beat and stone 300 elderly Bosnian Muslims.
- May 13 – Silvio Berlusconi wins the general election and becomes Prime Minister of Italy for the second time.
- May 14 – The Mac OS X Public Beta expires and its Aqua user interface ceases to function.
- May 22 – A large trans-Neptunian object (28978 Ixion) is found during the Deep Ecliptic Survey.
- May 22–23 – The Bahá'í Terraces officially open on Mount Carmel in Haifa, Israel (site of the Shrine of the Báb and the Bahá'í World Centre).

- May 24
  - Sherpa Temba Tsheri, 16, becomes the youngest person to summit Mount Everest.
  - The Versailles wedding hall disaster kills 23 in Jerusalem, Israel.

June

- June 1
  - Crown Prince Dipendra of Nepal kills his father, the king, his mother and other members of the royal family with an assault rifle and then shoots himself in the Nepalese royal massacre. Dipendra dies June 4, as King of Nepal. His uncle Gyanendra accedes to the throne.
  - A Hamas suicide bomber kills 21, mostly teenagers, in the Dolphinarium disco in Tel Aviv, Israel.
- June 5–9 – Tropical Storm Allison produces 36 inches (900 mm) of rain in Houston, killing 22, damaging the Texas Medical Center, and causing more than 5 billion American dollars of damage overall.
- June 7 – George W. Bush signs the Economic Growth and Tax Relief Reconciliation Act of 2001, the first tax cut of a series now known as the Bush tax cuts.
- June 11 – In Terre Haute, Indiana, Timothy McVeigh is executed for the Oklahoma City bombing.
- June 19 – A missile hits a soccer field in northern Iraq (Tel Afr County), killing 23 and wounding 11. According to U.S. officials, it was an Iraqi missile that malfunctioned.
- June 20 – Andrea Yates drowns all 5 of her young children in Houston, as a way to save them from Satan.
- June 21 – The world's longest train is set up by BHP Iron Ore and is recorded going between Newman and Port Hedland in Western Australia (a distance of 275 km, or 170 miles) and the train consists of 682 loaded iron ore wagons and 8 GE AC6000CW locomotives, giving a gross weight of almost 100,000 tonnes and moves 82,262 tonnes of ore; the train is 7.353 km (4.569 mi) long.

- June 23 – The 8.4 Mw southern Peru earthquake shakes coastal Peru with a maximum Mercalli intensity of VIII (*Severe*). A destructive tsunami followed, leaving at least 74 people dead, and 2,687 injured.

July

- July 2 – The world's first self-contained artificial heart is implanted in Robert Tools in the United States.
- July 3 – Vladivostok Air Flight 352 crashes on approach to landing at Irkutsk Airport, Russia, killing 145.
- July 7 – 2001 Bradford riots: Race riots erupt in Bradford in the north of England after National Front members reportedly stab an Asian man outside a pub.
- July 16
  - The People's Republic of China and the Russian Federation sign the 2001 Sino-Russian Treaty of Friendship ("Treaty of Good-Neighborliness and Friendly Cooperation").
  - The FBI arrests Dmitry Sklyarov at a convention in Las Vegas for violating a provision of the Digital Millennium Copyright Act.
- July 18 – In Baltimore, Maryland, a 60-car train derailment occurs in a tunnel, sparking a fire that lasts days and virtually shuts down downtown Baltimore.
- July 19 – UK politician and novelist Jeffrey Archer is sentenced to 4 years in prison for perjury and perverting the course of justice.
- July 20–22 – The 27th G8 summit takes place in Genoa, Italy. Massive demonstrations are held against the meeting by members of the anti-globalization movement. One demonstrator, Carlo Giuliani, is shot dead by a carabiniere. Several others are badly injured during a police attack on a school used by the protesters as their headquarters.
- July 24
  - Bandaranaike Airport attack: Tamil Tigers attack Bandaranaike International Airport in Sri Lanka, causing an estimated $500 million of damage.

- Simeon Saxe-Coburg-Gotha, deposed as the last Tsar of Bulgaria when a child, is sworn in as the democratically elected 48th Prime Minister of Bulgaria.

August

- August 1 – Alabama Supreme Court Chief Justice Roy Moore has a Ten Commandments monument installed in the judiciary building, leading to a lawsuit to have it removed and his own removal from office.
- August 6 – Erwadi fire incident, 28 mentally ill persons tied to chain were burnt to death at a faith based institution at Erwadi, Tamil Nadu.
- August 9 – Sbarro Restaurant in Jerusalem is attacked by a Palestinian militant, who kills 15 civilians and wounds 130.
- August 10 – The 2001 Angola train attack, causing 252 deaths.
- August 21 – NATO decides to send a peace-keeping force to the former Yugoslav Republic of Macedonia.
- August 24 – Air Transat Flight 236 runs out of fuel over the Atlantic Ocean (en route to Lisbon from Toronto) and makes an emergency landing in the Azores.
- August 25 – American singer Aaliyah and several members of her record company are killed as their overloaded aircraft crashes shortly after takeoff from Marsh Harbour Airport, Bahamas.
- August 31 – September 1 – The 2001 Vancouver TV realignment occurs in British Columbia, Canada.
- August 31 – The World Conference against Racism 2001 begins in Durban, South Africa.

September

September 11 attacks

- September – The piece As Slow as Possible, composed by John Cage, begins. It will last 639 years, finishing in the year 2640.
- September 3
  - In Belfast, Protestant loyalists begin a picket of Holy Cross, a Catholic primary school for girls. For the next 11 weeks, riot police escort the schoolchildren and their parents through hundreds of protesters, amid rioting and heightened violence.
  - The United States, Canada and Israel withdraw from the U.N. Conference on Racism because they feel that the issue of Zionism is overemphasized.
- September 4 – Tokyo DisneySea opens to the public as part of the Tokyo Disney Resort in Urayasu, Chiba, Japan.
- September 6 – *United States v. Microsoft Corp.*: The United States Justice Department announces that it no longer seeks to break up software maker Microsoft, and will instead seek a lesser antitrust penalty.
- September 9
  - A suicide bomber kills Ahmad Shah Massoud, military commander of the Afghan Northern Alliance.
  - 68 people die of methanol poisoning in Pärnu County, Estonia.
  - The Unix billennium is reached, marking the beginning of the use of 10-digit decimal Unix time stamps.
  -

- September 10
  - Donald Rumsfeld gives a speech regarding $2.3 trillion in Pentagon spending that cannot be accounted for. He identifies the Pentagon bureaucracy as the biggest threat to America.
  - Antônio da Costa Santos, mayor of Campinas, Brazil is assassinated.
- September 11 – 2,996 victims are killed in the September 11 attacks at the World Trade Center in New York City, New York, The Pentagon in Arlington County, Virginia, and in rural Shanksville, Pennsylvania after American Airlines Flight 11 and United Airlines Flight 175 are hijacked and crash into the World Trade Center's Twin Towers, American Airlines Flight 77 is hijacked and crashes into the Pentagon, and United Airlines Flight 93 is hijacked and crashes into grassland in Shanksville, due to the passengers fighting to regain control of the airplane. The World Trade Center towers collapse as a result of the crashes.
- September 12 – Ansett Australia Airlines is placed into administration, the company's fleet is grounded 2 days later on September 14.
- September 13 – Civilian aircraft traffic resumes in the United States after the September 11 attacks.
- September 14 – Historic National Prayer Service held at Washington National Cathedral for victims of the September 11 attacks. A similar service is held in Canada on Parliament Hill, the largest vigil ever held in the nation's capital.
- September 17 – The New York Stock Exchange reopens for trading after the September 11 attacks, the longest closure since the Great Depression.
- September 18 – The 2001 anthrax attacks commence as letters containing anthrax spores are mailed from Princeton, New Jersey to ABC News, CBS News, NBC News, the *New York Post*, and the *National Enquirer*. 22 in total are exposed; 5 of them die.
- September 20 – In an address to a joint session of Congress and the American people, U.S. President George W. Bush declares a "War on Terror".

- September 21
  - In Toulouse, France, the AZote Fertilisant chemical factory explodes, killing 29 and seriously wounding over 2,500.
  - Deep Space 1 flies within 2,200 km of Comet Borrelly.
  - America: A Tribute to Heroes is broadcast by over 35 network and cable channels, raising over $200 million for the victims of the September 11 attacks.
- September 27 – Zug massacre: In Zug, Switzerland, Friedrich Leibacher shoots 18 citizens, killing 14 and then himself.

October

- October 1 – Militants attack the state legislature building in Srinagar, Kashmir, killing 38.
- October 2 – Swissair seeks for bankruptcy protection and grounds its entire fleet, resulting in over 230 flights cancelled and stranding 18,000 people worldwide.
- October 4 – Siberia Airlines Flight 1812 crashes over the Black Sea en route from Tel Aviv, Israel, to Novosibirsk, Russia; 78 are killed.
- October 7 – War in Afghanistan: The United States invades Afghanistan, with participation from other nations.
- October 8
  - A twin engine Cessna and Scandinavian Airlines jetliner collide in heavy fog during takeoff from Milan, Italy, killing 118 people.
  - U.S. President George W. Bush announces the establishment of the Office of Homeland Security.
- October 9 – Second mailing of anthrax letters from Trenton, New Jersey in the 2001 anthrax attacks.
- October 11 – The Polaroid Corporation files for federal bankruptcy protection.
- October 15 – NASA's Galileo spacecraft passes within 112 miles (180 km) of Jupiter's moon Io.
- October 17 – Israeli tourism minister Rehavam Ze'evi becomes the first Israeli minister to be assassinated in a terrorist attack.

- October 19 – *SIEV X* sinks en route to Christmas Island, killing 353 people.
- October 22 – *Grand Theft Auto III* is released, popularizing a genre of open-world, action-adventure video games as well as spurring controversy around violence in video games.
- October 23
  - The Provisional Irish Republican Army of Northern Ireland commences disarmament after peace talks.
  - The iPod is first introduced by Apple.
- October 25 – Microsoft releases Windows XP.
- October 26 – U.S. President George W. Bush signs the Patriot Act into law.

November

Soldiers board a Chinook helicopter

- November 2 – The Glocal Forum, leading international organization in the field of city-to-city cooperation, is established by Ambassador Uri Savir.
- November 4
  - Hurricane Michelle hits Cuba, destroying crops and thousands of homes.
  - The Police Service of Northern Ireland is established, replacing the controversial Royal Ulster Constabulary.
- November 7 – Sabena, the national airline of Belgium, goes bankrupt.
- November 10
  - The People's Republic of China is admitted to the World Trade Organization after 15 years of negotiations.

- Heavy rains and mudslides in Algeria kill more than 900.
- John Howard, the Prime Minister of Australia, is elected to a third term.
- November 11 – Journalists Pierre Billaud, Johanne Sutton and Volker Handloik are killed in Afghanistan during an attack on the convoy they are traveling in.
- November 12
  - American Airlines Flight 587 crashes in Queens minutes after takeoff from John F. Kennedy International Airport, killing all 260 on board.
  - War in Afghanistan: Taliban forces abandon Kabul, ahead of advancing Northern Alliance troops.
- November 13 – In the first such act since World War II, U.S. President George W. Bush signs an executive order allowing military tribunals against any foreigners suspected of having connections to terrorist acts or planned acts against the United States.
- November 14 – War in Afghanistan: Northern Alliance fighters take over the capital Kabul.
- November 20 – U.S. President George W. Bush dedicates the United States Department of Justice headquarters building as the Robert F. Kennedy Justice Building, honoring the late Robert F. Kennedy on what would have been his 76th birthday.
- November 23 – The Convention on Cybercrime is signed in Budapest, Hungary.
- November 27 – A hydrogen atmosphere is discovered on the extrasolar planet Osiris by the Hubble Space Telescope, the first atmosphere detected on an extrasolar planet.
- November 30 – Gary Ridgway, a.k.a. The Green River Killer, is arrested outside of the truck factory where he had worked in Renton, Washington. His arrest marked the end of one of the longest running homicide investigations in US history.

December

- December 1 – The last Trans World Airlines flight lands at St. Louis International Airport, following TWA's purchase by American Airlines.
- December 2
  - Enron files for Chapter 11 bankruptcy protection 5 days after Dynegy cancels a US$8.4 billion buyout bid (to this point, the largest bankruptcy in U.S. history).
  - 1998–2002 Argentine great depression: *Corralito* – The government effectively freezes all bank accounts for twelve months leading to December 2001 riots in Argentina.
- December 3 – Officials announce that one of the Taliban prisoners captured after the prison uprising at Mazar-i-Sharif, Afghanistan is John Walker Lindh, a United States citizen.
- December 11
  - The People's Republic of China joins the World Trade Organization.
  - The United States government indicts Zacarias Moussaoui for involvement in the September 11 attacks.
  - The United States Customs Service raids members of international software piracy group DrinkOrDie in Operation Buccaneer.
- December 13
  - 2001 Indian Parliament attack: 12 are killed, leading to a 2001–02 India–Pakistan standoff.
  - U.S. President George W. Bush announces the US withdrawal from the 1972 Anti-Ballistic Missile Treaty.
- December 15 – The Leaning Tower of Pisa reopens after 11 years and $27,000,000 spent to fortify it, without fixing its famous lean.
- December 19
  - A record high barometric pressure of 1085.6 hPa (32.06 inHg) is recorded at Tosontsengel, Khövsgöl, Mongolia.
  - Argentine economic crisis: December riots: Riots erupt in Buenos Aires, Argentina.
  -

- December 22
  - Burhanuddin Rabbani, political leader of the Northern Alliance, hands over power in Afghanistan to the interim government headed by President Hamid Karzai.
  - Richard Reid attempts to destroy a passenger airliner by igniting explosives hidden in his shoes aboard American Airlines Flight 63.
- December 27
  - The People's Republic of China is granted permanent normal trade status with the United States.
  - Tropical Storm Vamei forms within 1.5 degrees of the equator. No other tropical cyclone in recorded history has come as close to the equator.
- December 29 – A fire at the Mesa Redonda shopping center in Lima, Peru, kills at least 291.

Births

January

- January 21 – Jackson Brundage, American actor

February

- February 2 – Connor Gibbs, American actor
- February 5 – Juan Karlos Labajo, Filipino singer and performer
- February 15 – Haley Tju, American actress
- February 19 – David Mazouz, American actor
- February 20 – Ren Qian, Chinese diver
- February 24 – Ramona Marquez, British actress

April

- April 8 - Kyla Rae Kowalewski, American actress

May

- May 24 – Darren Espanto, Filipino singer and performer

June

- June 21 – Eleanor Worthington Cox, British actress

July

- July 10 – Isabela Moner, American actress

August

- August 23 – Zaijian Jaranilla, Filipino actor

September

- September 4 – Tenzing Norgay Trainor, American actor

October

- October 12 – Raymond Ochoa, American actor
- October 14 – Rowan Blanchard, American actress
- October 25 – Princess Elisabeth, Duchess of Brabant, daughter and Heiress Apparent of Philippe, King of the Belgians

November

- November 21 – Samantha Bailey, American actress
- November 27 – Morgana Davies, Australian actress

December

- December 1 – Aiko, Princess Toshi of Japan
- December 14 - Joshua Rush, American actor
- December 28 – Madison De La Garza, American actress

Deaths

January

Marie José of Belgium

- January 1 – Ray Walston, American actor (b. 1914)
- January 12
  - William Redington Hewlett, American businessman (b. 1913)
  - Adhemar da Silva, Brazilian athlete (b. 1927)
- January 16
  - Virginia O'Brien, American actress (b. 1919)
  - Laurent-Désiré Kabila, president of the Democratic Republic of the Congo (b. 1939)
- January 27 – Marie José of Belgium, last Queen of Italy (b. 1906)
- January 30 – Michel Marcel Navratil, last French citizen and male survivor of the Titanic disaster (b. 1908)
- January 31 – Gordon R. Dickson, Canadian writer (b. 1923)

February

Dale Earnhardt

Stanley Kramer

- February 4 – Iannis Xenakis, Greek composer (b. 1922)
- February 7 – King Moody, American actor (b. 1929)
- February 9 – Herbert A. Simon, American economist, Nobel Prize laureate (b. 1916)
- February 18
  - Balthus, French painter (b. 1908)
  - Dale Earnhardt, American auto racing driver (b. 1951)
- February 19
  - Stanley Kramer, American film director (b. 1913)
  - Charles Trenet, French singer (b. 1913)
- February 20 – Rosemary DeCamp, American actress (b. 1910)
- February 24 – Claude Shannon, American mathematician (b. 1916)
- February 25 – Sir Donald Bradman, Australian cricketer (b. 1908)

March

Ann Sothern

- March 12
  - Morton Downey, Jr., American television personality (b. 1932)
  - Robert Ludlum, American author (b. 1927)
  -

- March 15
  - Gaetano Cozzi, Italian historian (b. 1922)
  - Ann Sothern, American actress (b. 1909)
- March 18 – John Phillips, American singer/songwriter (b. 1935)
- March 22 – William Hanna, American animator and businessman (b. 1910)
- March 31 – Clifford Shull, American physicist, Nobel Prize laureate (b. 1915)

April

Joey Ramone

- April 7 – David Graf, American actor (b. 1950)
- April 8 – Van Stephenson, American singer-songwriter (b. 1953)
- April 15 – Joey Ramone, American musician and singer (b. 1951)
- April 20 – Giuseppe Sinopoli, Italian conductor and composer (b. 1946)
- April 21 – Jack Haley Jr., American film director and producer (b. 1933)
- April 26 – Michele Alboreto, Italian racing driver (b. 1956)
- April 29 – Barend Biesheuvel, Dutch politician and corporate director, Prime Minister of the Netherlands (1971–1973) (b. 1920)

May

Douglas Adams

- May 11 – Douglas Adams, English author (b. 1952)
- May 12 – Perry Como, American singer (b. 1912)
- May 13 – R. K. Narayan, Indian novelist (b. 1906)
- May 17 – Jacques-Louis Lions, French mathematician (b. 1928)
- May 24 – Javier Urruticoechea, Spanish footballer (b. 1952)
- May 31 – Arlene Francis, American actress and game show panelist (b. 1907)

June

Anthony Quinn

Jack Lemmon

- June 1 – King Birendra of Nepal (b. 1945)
- June 2 – Imogene Coca, American actress (b. 1908)
- June 3 – Anthony Quinn, Mexican-American actor (b. 1915)
- June 4 – King Dipendra of Nepal (b. 1971)
- June 7 – Víctor Paz Estenssoro, President of Bolivia (b. 1907)
- June 10 – Leila Pahlavi, Iranian princess (b. 1970)
- June 17 – Donald J. Cram, American chemist, Nobel Prize laureate (b. 1919)
- June 21
  - John Lee Hooker, American musician (b. 1917)
  - Carroll O'Connor, American actor (b. 1924)
- June 27
  - Tove Jansson, Finnish author (b. 1914)
  - Jack Lemmon, American actor and director (b. 1925)
- June 28
  - Joan Sims, English actress (b. 1930)
  - Mortimer J. Adler, American philosopher (b. 1902)
- June 30 – Chet Atkins, American guitarist and record producer (b. 1924)

July

Edward Gierek

- July 1 – Nikolay Basov, Soviet physicist, Nobel Prize laureate (b. 1922)
- July 11 – Gaspare di Mercurio, Italian doctor and author (b. 1926)
- July 24 – Hiroshi Tsuburaya, Japanese actor (b. 1964)
- July 28 – Ahmed Sofa, Bangladeshi writer (b. 1943)
- July 29 – Edward Gierek, Polish politician (b. 1913)

August

7th Earl of Longford

Jane Greer

- August 1 – Poul Anderson, American author (b. 1926)
- August 3 – Frank Pakenham, 7th Earl of Longford, British peer, politician and reformer (b. 1905)
- August 4 – Lorenzo Music, American voice actor (b. 1937)
- August 6
  - Larry Adler, American musician (b. 1914)
  - Jorge Amado, Brazilian writer (b. 1912)
- August 20 – Fred Hoyle, British astronomer and writer (b. 1915)
- August 22 – Bernard Heuvelmans, Belgian-French cryptozoologist (b. 1916)
- August 23 – Kathleen Freeman, American actress (b. 1919)
- August 24 – Jane Greer, American actress (b. 1924)
- August 25
  - Ken Tyrrell, British auto racing driver (b. 1924)
  - Aaliyah, R&B singer and actress (b. 1979)

September

Troy Donahue

Dorothy McGuire

- September 2
  - Christiaan Barnard, South African surgeon (b. 1922)
  - Troy Donahue, American actor (b. 1936)
- September 3
  - Pauline Kael, American film critic (b. 1919)
  - Thuy Trang, Vietnamese American actress (b. 1973)
- September 9 – Ahmad Shah Massoud, Afghan military commander (b. 1953)
- September 11 – 2,996 people (2,977 victims and 19 hijackers) who died in the September 11 attacks
  - David Angell, American television producer (b. 1946)
  - Berry Berenson, American photographer (and widow of Anthony Perkins) (b. 1948)
  - Barbara Olson, American television commentator (b. 1955)
- September 12 – Victor Wong, Chinese-American character actor (b. 1927)
- September 13 – Frédéric-Antonin Breysse, French cartoonist (b. 1907)
- September 14 – Dorothy McGuire, American actress (b. 1916)

- September 20
  - Marcos Pérez Jiménez, former President of Venezuela (b. 1914)
  - Karl-Eduard von Schnitzler, East German journalist and host of the television show Der schwarze Kanal (b. 1918)
- September 22 – Isaac Stern, Ukrainian violinist (b. 1920)

October

Zhang Xueliang

- October 4 – Blaise Alexander, American automobile racing driver (b. 1976)
- October 15 – Zhang Xueliang, Chinese military figure (b. 1901)
- October 22 – Bertie Mee, English football player and coach (b. 1918)
- October 24 – Jaromil Jireš, Czechoslovak filmmaker (b. 1935)

November

George Harrison

- November 3 – Sir Ernst Hans Josef Gombrich, OM, CBE, Austrian-born art historian (b. 1909)

- November 9 – Giovanni Leone, former Prime Minister of Italy (b. 1908)
- November 10 – Ken Kesey, American author (b. 1935)
- November 24
  - Melanie Thornton, American singer (La Bouche) (b. 1967)
  - Rachel Gurney, British actress (b. 1920)
- November 25 – Gohar Shahi, Pakistani spiritual leader (b. 1941)
- November 29
  - George Harrison, English musician (The Beatles) (b. 1943)
  - John Mitchum, American actor (b. 1919)

December

Léopold Sédar Senghor

- December 12 – Josef Bican, Czech-Austrian footballer (b. 1913)
- December 13 – Chuck Schuldiner, American singer and guitarist (b. 1967)
- December 16 – Stuart Adamson, Scottish singer and guitarist (Big Country) (b. 1958)
- December 18 – Marcel Mule, French saxophonist (b. 1901)
- December 20 – Léopold Sédar Senghor, First president of Senegal (b. 1906)
- December 22
  - Grzegorz Ciechowski, Polish musician (b. 1957)
  - Walter Newton Read, American lawyer and second chairman of the New Jersey Casino Control Commission (b. 1918)
- December 23 – Jelle Zijlstra, Dutch politician and economist, Prime Minister of the Netherlands (1966–1967) (b. 1918)
- December 26 – Nigel Hawthorne, British actor (b. 1929)

Specific date of death unknown

- Etan Patz was declared legally dead. He was an American child that disappeared on May 25, 1979. His disappearance sparked the missing children's movement.

Nobel Prizes

- Physics – Eric Allin Cornell, Wolfgang Ketterle, and Carl Wieman
- Chemistry – William Standish Knowles, Ryōji Noyori, and Karl Barry Sharpless
- Medicine – Leland H. Hartwell, Tim Hunt, and Paul Nurse
- Literature – V. S. Naipaul
- Peace – United Nations, Kofi Annan
- Bank of Sweden Prize in Economic Sciences in Memory of Alfred Nobel – George Akerlof, Michael Spence, and Joseph Stiglitz

In the News

2001 becomes known as "Summer of the Shark" after a number of shark attack fatalities.

IRA Dismantles it's weapons arsenal after years of fighting.

Known simply as 9/11. On September 11, 2001 Nineteen hijackers simultaneously took control of four U.S. domestic commercial airliners. The hijackers crashed two planes into the World Trade Center in Manhattan, New York City one into each of the two tallest towers. Within two hours, both towers collapsed. The hijackers crashed the third aircraft into the U.S. Department of Defense headquarters, the Pentagon, in Arlington County, Virginia. The fourth plane crashed into a rural field in Somerset County, Pennsylvania, following apparent passenger resistance.

The United States invades Afghanistan, with some participation from the UK. Marking the beginning of the US "War on Terrorism"

Dennis Tito becomes the first space tourist during May of 2001.

A series of Anthrax attacks spreads fear amongst the American Public and several people are infected by handling infected letters.

The Leaning Tower of Pisa reopens after 11 years repairs to stop it falling over.

Apple Computer releases the iPod.

Popular Films - Harry Potter and the Philosopher's Stone, The Lord of the Rings: The Fellowship of the Ring, Monsters, Inc, Shrek, Ocean's Eleven, Pearl Harbor, The Mummy Returns, Jurassic Park III.

2001 Calendar

January 2001

Sun	Mon	Tue	Wed	Thu	Fri	Sat
	1	2	3	4	5	6
7	8	9	10	11	12	13
14	15	16	17	18	19	20
21	22	23	24	25	26	27
28	29	30	31			

February 2001

Sun	Mon	Tue	Wed	Thu	Fri	Sat
				1	2	3
4	5	6	7	8	9	10
11	12	13	14	15	16	17
18	19	20	21	22	23	24
25	26	27	28			

March 2001

Sun	Mon	Tue	Wed	Thu	Fri	Sat
				1	2	3
4	5	6	7	8	9	10
11	12	13	14	15	16	17
18	19	20	21	22	23	24
25	26	27	28	29	30	31

April 2001

Sun	Mon	Tue	Wed	Thu	Fri	Sat
1	2	3	4	5	6	7
8	9	10	11	12	13	14
15	16	17	18	19	20	21
22	23	24	25	26	27	28
29	30					

May 2001

Sun	Mon	Tue	Wed	Thu	Fri	Sat
		1	2	3	4	5
6	7	8	9	10	11	12
13	14	15	16	17	18	19
20	21	22	23	24	25	26
27	28	29	30	31		

June 2001

Sun	Mon	Tue	Wed	Thu	Fri	Sat
					1	2
3	4	5	6	7	8	9
10	11	12	13	14	15	16
17	18	19	20	21	22	23
24	25	26	27	28	29	30

July 2001

Sun	Mon	Tue	Wed	Thu	Fri	Sat
1	2	3	4	5	6	7
8	9	10	11	12	13	14
15	16	17	18	19	20	21
22	23	24	25	26	27	28
29	30	31				

August 2001

Sun	Mon	Tue	Wed	Thu	Fri	Sat
			1	2	3	4
5	6	7	8	9	10	11
12	13	14	15	16	17	18
19	20	21	22	23	24	25
26	27	28	29	30	31	

September 2001

Sun	Mon	Tue	Wed	Thu	Fri	Sat
						1
2	3	4	5	6	7	8
9	10	11	12	13	14	15
16	17	18	19	20	21	22
23	24	25	26	27	28	29
30						

October 2001

Sun	Mon	Tue	Wed	Thu	Fri	Sat
	1	2	3	4	5	6
7	8	9	10	11	12	13
14	15	16	17	18	19	20
21	22	23	24	25	26	27
28	29	30	31			

November 2001

Sun	Mon	Tue	Wed	Thu	Fri	Sat
				1	2	3
4	5	6	7	8	9	10
11	12	13	14	15	16	17
18	19	20	21	22	23	24
25	26	27	28	29	30	

December 2001

Sun	Mon	Tue	Wed	Thu	Fri	Sat
						1
2	3	4	5	6	7	8
9	10	11	12	13	14	15
16	17	18	19	20	21	22
23	24	25	26	27	28	29
30	31					

www.ingramcontent.com/pod-product-compliance
Lightning Source LLC
Chambersburg PA
CBHW070249290526
45789CB00004B/1814